Where do peanuts look like teddy bears
Or the carousel horses you ride at fairs?
In Look-Alike Land! That magical spot
Where everyday things look like what they're not.
A balloon is a dress? Pistachios are flowers?
Look-alikes can keep you looking for hours.
More than one hundred objects in each scene (but two) –
Find some or ALL. It's up to you.
(For you puzzle hounds who like to keep track,
A complete list of look-alikes appears at the back.)

So come with me – I'll be your guide
To all the wonders you'll see inside…

SUPER
LOOK-ALIKES™

WALKER BOOKS
AND SUBSIDIARIES
LONDON • BOSTON • SYDNEY

First published 1998 by Little, Brown and Company, USA

First published in Great Britain 2001 by Walker Books Ltd
87 Vauxhall Walk, London SE11 5HJ

This edition published 2002

2 4 6 8 10 9 7 5 3 1

© 1998 Joan Steiner
Photography by Thomas Lindley

The General Store scene was photographed by Walter Wick
The Neighbourhood scene was photographed by Jeff Heiges

This book has been typeset in Futura and ATGoudy

Printed in Hong Kong

British Library Cataloguing in Publication Data:
a catalogue record for this book
is available from the British Library

ISBN 0-7445-8953-3

Come along! Jump aboard! Grab hold of my hand.
We're crossing the border into Look-Alike Land.
Everything's changing! Believe it or not,
It looks like this engine's a huge COFFEE-POT!

Our long trip is over. The train's in the station.
It's time to use your imagination!
Start searching for look-alikes right in this tunnel.
See the top of the news-stand? It looks like a FUNNEL.

Out of the station and into the light,
Look-Alike City's a magical sight!
And the look-alikes keep getting better and better.
I see a building that looks like a SWEATER.

While we're in town, let's visit the shop
That's packed full of look-alikes, bottom to top.
Buy a RAZOR that vacuums to keep your house neat,
Or a lamp that looks like a PEPPERMINT SWEET.

We'll start our tour with the park and the zoo.
Let's search for look-alikes while strolling through.
Here's one that isn't often seen –
A sandpit that looks like a TAMBOURINE.

I'm so excited! Look-Alike Fair is in town!
It's a great place to go when the sun's going down.
Look-alikes spinning – twirlers, whirlers and whizzers,
And a huge Ferris wheel that looks just like SCISSORS.

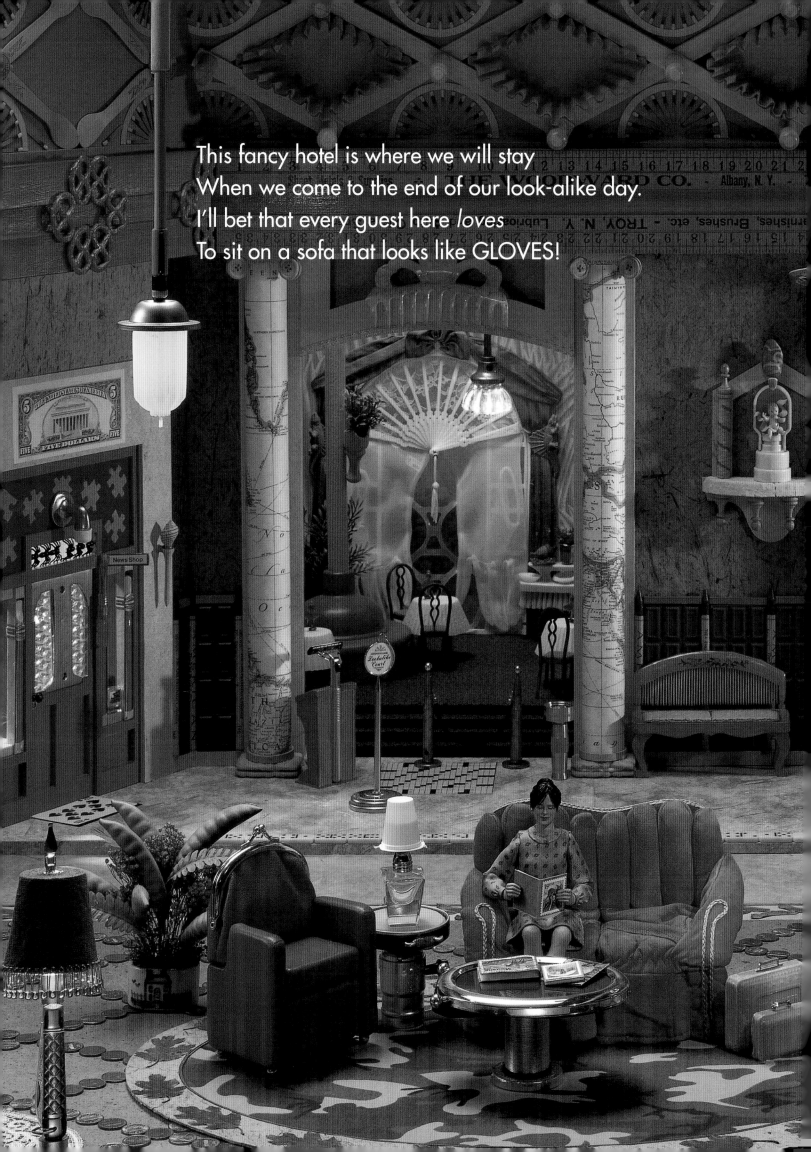

This fancy hotel is where we will stay
When we come to the end of our look-alike day.
I'll bet that every guest here *loves*
To sit on a sofa that looks like GLOVES!

Up bright and early, let's visit a street
Where the houses look good enough to eat.
And not *just* the houses – as you can see,
The bushes look just like BROCCOLI.

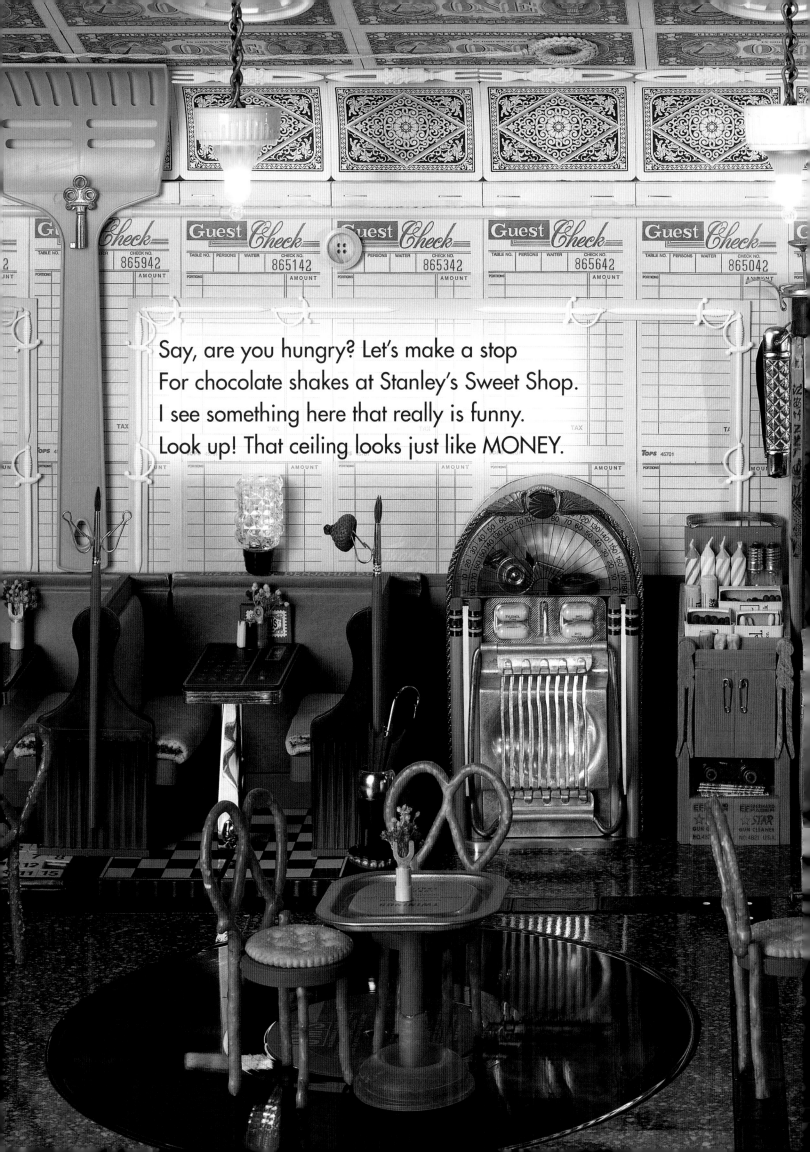

Say, are you hungry? Let's make a stop
For chocolate shakes at Stanley's Sweet Shop.
I see something here that really is funny.
Look up! That ceiling looks just like MONEY.

And now for an extra-special treat:
The Look-Alike Circus, front-row seat!
The clown is so funny – his outfit's so quaint
With trousers that look like two TUBES OF PAINT.

The time has come to sail away.
But please come back another day.
Down by the harbour, we'll say "Farewell!"
And ring you out on the big COW BELL.

EXTRA CHALLENGE

Let's scan every scene again
For *two* things that start with P-E-N.
One is something you can spend;
The other sharpens at the end.
On every page they can be found.
Did you spot them first time round?

HOW TO COUNT THE LOOK-ALIKES

1. If more than one of the same object is used to make up *one* look-alike (such as ten pencils making up a fence), it counts as *one* look-alike. But if the same or a similar object appears elsewhere in the scene to make a *different* look-alike (such as a pencil appearing as a flagpole), it counts again.

2. Miniatures don't count as look-alikes unless they appear as something different from a larger version of themselves. For example, a toy car that represents a real car is not a look-alike. But a toy car that looks like a fire hydrant *does* count.

3. As long as you can identify an object, you don't have to get the name exactly right.

THE LOOK-ALIKES

Asterisks indicate hard-to-find items – for super-sleuths only!

TRAIN

• *132 Look-alikes*

LOCOMOTIVE: Front of engine: coffee-pot, overalls buckle, bingo call number, nuts (nut-and-bolt type). **Cowcatcher:** toy truck, harmonica, nail clipper, red cocktail fork, package carrying handle, red birthday candle. **Lower engine and wheels:** cap guns, roll of film, battery, black ballpoint pen lid*, toy handcuffs, wristwatch face, toy compass, pair of compasses with pencil, book of matches, can-opener, green pencil-top rubber, spanners, cat-food cans, bottle tops, (more bingo call numbers), spark plug, tyre pressure gauge, die, small calculator, confectionery thermometer, hacksaw, pencil-sharpener, buckle, bottle stopper, pencil, felt-tip marker, stock cubes. **Upper engine:** spool of thread, postage stamp, Slinky, sink plug, small jar of honey, knitting-needle, green button, electrical connectors (holding knitting-needle), sewing needles in paper. **Cab:** child's sandals, carpenter's clamp, pushpins, subway token, hinge, photographic slide, big safety-pin, old-fashioned keys. **REST OF TRAIN: Coal carrier:** purse, green padlock, two books, toy car, ballpoint pen refill, corkscrew/bottle-opener, can/bottle-opener, jar tops*, sewing-machine bobbins. **Freight car:** cardboard box, steak knives, swizzle-sticks, spiral notepads, rubber bands, balsa aeroplane parts, toy pilot's wings*, toothpick, wooden match, crochet hook, twist ties, price-tag, orange ticket, tape measure, tiny plastic clothes-peg, small clasp envelopes, orange cocktail forks, theatre ticket voucher, green comb, domino*, green magnetic letters, key holder, bulldog paper-clips*, dollar bill. **Passenger car:** six-pack box, green toothbrush*, green pick-up stick, penny, six-inch ruler, paintbrush*, watch strap, half-dollars*, paper-clip, carpenter's clamp*, razors (steps)*, ring, luggage tag*, toy wooden animal. **WATER TOWER:** Sifter, dollar bill, wooden cocktail forks, chopsticks, whisk, rubber stamp handle, needle and thread, weighted fish-hook. **TRACKS, OVERPASS AND FOREGROUND:** Screwdriver, TV antenna, chopstick*, cinnamon sticks, grater*, twelve-inch ruler, jigsaw puzzle pieces, stapler, guitar case, pine cones, potatoes, pecans. **SMOKE AND SKY:** Cotton wool, white rose, toy bunny, baby bootie, pearl earring, baby tooth, jingle bell, button, acorn, seashell, pearl, popper.

TRAIN STATION

• *78 Look-alikes*

FOREGROUND AND CEILING: Keys, windscreen wipers, dominoes, torch, kazoo, badminton racquets, embroidery hoops, hangers, scissors, clothes-pegs, wooden fork, juicer. **UPPER PLATFORM LEVEL: Back wall:** paintbrushes, jingle bells, chopsticks, spring-type clothes-pegs, silverware organizer trays, plastic spoon, spiral notepad, pocket calculator. **Snack bar:** toothbrushes, travel toothbrush holder, clear plastic ruler, artist's blending stick, paper-clips, stamp*, pick-up stick, magnifying glass, sticks of chewing-gum*, high-heeled doll's shoes*. **Ticket booth:** thermometers, pearl earrings, supermarket bonus stamps, dollar bills. **Waiting room:** vegetable steamer, egg slicer, cigarettes, nail clippers, hair-clip, weighted fish-hooks, small screwdriver. **Information booth:** baby-bottle teat, white chess pawns. **Railing and gates:** dry-wall screws, binder clips, tape measure, black crayon. **LOWER PLATFORMS:** Disposable razors, pen nibs, funnel, matchbox. **Train:** lipstick, wallet, birthday candles, photographic slides, penny, retractable measuring tape, chocolate-covered marsh-mallow cookies, rubber tap attachment, whistle, fondue fork, nut (nut-and-bolt type), thermos, shoe polish tins, spanner, pair of compasses with pencil, nine-volt battery, C battery. **Baggage cart:** matches, bingo call number, poppers, peanuts, die, cough-drop in wrapper, Tootsie Roll cake, caramels, Scrabble tiles, eye (hook-and-eye type).

LOOK-ALIKE CITY

• *207 Look-alikes*

CANOPY: Garden rake, bullets, Christmas bauble. **BUILDINGS TO LEFT OF CROSSROADS: Building at far left:** felt-tip pen, drinking straw, old cookbook. **Building on left-hand corner:** green suitcase, mousetraps, pistachio nuts (red and natural), toy trumpet Christmas ornament, staple remover, pastels, honey dippers, recorders, handcuffs, cupcake cases, bottle cap, toothbrush-and-cup holder, craft knives, pearl earrings, blue crayons, tube of paint, hook (hook-and-eye type)*, uninflated pink balloon, drill bit, travel soap-dish with soap, pearl anklet, Smarties, spools of thread, roll of cap-gun caps, birthday-candle holder, sticks of chewing-gum*, whistle, price stickers, doll's shoes, toy wooden geese, cap guns, nuts and bolts. **BUILDINGS AND THINGS SEEN THROUGH CROSSROADS: Bus:** carpenter's clamp, audio cassette, clear button*. **Building behind bus:** champagne cork, rubber stamp, Scrabble tile, baseball card*, paint stirring stick. **Blue-roofed building and behind it:** snooker-cue chalk, matchboxes, phone jack, blue pencil-tip rubbers, spiral notepad, posable sculptor's mannequin, salt-shaker top, hourglass egg-timers, ballpoint pen and holder, folding carpenter's ruler*, wafer biscuits. **Church:** pen nibs, brown pencils,

chocolate chips, metronome, chess king, wedding ring*, penny, purse, small bottles, chess pawns, hair-grip*, file folders, newspaper, plastic cocktail forks, tape measure, buttons, pecans, breakfast cereal hexagons. **Truck:** packets of sewing needles. **In crossroads:** punch-type can-opener, M&Ms, pairs of compasses, pearls, small yellow pencils, fishing line weights, clothing label, small chalkboard, lentils. **RESTAURANT BUILDING:** Book, bell, chess bishops, paintbrushes, alphabet spaghetti, nutcracker, cable-knit sweater, black-eyed peas, fancy toothpicks, sweetcorn kernels, pushpins, pretzels, peanut, safety-pins, clothes-pegs, price-tags, dollar bills, book of matches, blue birthday candles, silver dollars (tables), electrical connectors (vases)*, champagne cork cages, paper-clips, melba toasts. **Signpost on corner:** glass cutter. **DELICATESSEN BUILDING:** Supermarket bonus stamps, jigsaw puzzle piece, cigarillo, ruler, shade pull, dried maple-seed cases, crackers, chopsticks, incense sticks, gum rubbers, wool label, postage stamps, paint-chip strip, emery board, miniature watercolour kits, Cheerios, plastic protractor, pet collar, tiny buckles, luggage tag, diamond ring, thimbles, popcorn, nail clippers, drop earring, sweet in wrapper, pine cone, bingo game cards, alphabet blocks, yellow pencil-sharpener, spool of red thread, die, TinkerToy part, red stock cube*, seashell, button*, swizzle-stick, toy car. **Signposts in front of deli building:** machine screw, large nail, museum admission tag, digital watch face, bulldog paper-clip, bread closure tag, screwdriver, nut (nut-and-bolt type). **TOY SHOP BUILDING:** Shutter, Scrabble board, knitting-needles, cocktail forks, corn-on-the-cob holders, plastic bandage, red crayons, Chinese finger puzzle, hair clips, jack (from game of jacks), wooden matches, postage stamps, chess knight, hair-grips, sweetcorn kernels, pistachio nut, spiral pasta, seashell, ball-headed pin, cork, model train freight car (Note: Puppet, teddy bear and goose are miniatures rather than look-alikes.). **Hydrant:** roll of film, poppers, salt-shaker top. **CAR:** Black shoe, mushrooms, sewing needle, zip slide, acorn, silver hair-grips, key-chain clasp (door handle)*. **FOREGROUND AND STREET: From left:** scallop shell, shower-curtain hook, toy ring in plastic bubble from vending machine, tyre pressure gauge, popcorn, eggcup, dominoes, chessboard, lollipop, Oreo biscuit, coin, ceramic napkin ring, meat thermometer, coin, ice-cream cone, dress pattern (roadway), photographic slide (grating in road). **Figures in foreground:** white seashell, peanut.

GENERAL STORE

• *156 Look-alikes*

Note: This scene contains many doll's house miniatures and decorative ceramic beads (not counted as look-alikes).

CEILING AND HANGING FROM CEILING: Playing-cards, belt buckles, pull chain, sink plugs, key-ring, tiny padlocks, large nail, safety-pins, nutcracker, curtain hook*, sea urchin spine (far left salami), cigar ring (on second salami), tiny key on chain, tea ball, manicure scissors, hair clip, tea bags, lace, yardstick, pennies, key chain with metal tag. **BACK WALL: Doorway and window:** pretzels, white birthday candle (doorway window shade), photographic slides, plastic sleeve for slides, waistband hook (doorknob), pearl earrings, chopsticks, brown cigarettes, pocket comb, green Life Saver sweet, swizzle-stick, burnt matches, crystal decanter stopper*. **In front of door and window:** crossword puzzle, dice, cigar holder, bottle cap, bolt, small comb, melba toast, chess pieces. **Outside door and window:** peppermint stick*, meat thermometer*. **Shelf units:** pen nibs, pencils, (more chopsticks), clear ballpoint pens, crayon boxes, thermometer, scallop shell. **Shelves behind shopkeeper:** white chess rook, peppermint sweet, toothpaste tube caps, pencil-sharpeners, ballpoint pen refill, black sink plug, thimbles, fuse, whistle, roll of film. **Shelves behind deli case:** clear suction cup, cuff-link, car cigarette-lighter, brooch pin-back, electrical connectors, fruit sweet in wrapper, red draughts piece, cap-gun cap rolls, Rawlplugs, tiddlywinks*, caramel, salt and pepper shakers. **Remaining shelves:** gum rubbers, sugar-cubes, crochet hook, hook (hook-and-eye type), wrapped sticks of chewing-gum, bingo call numbers, bubble-gum (wrapped and unwrapped), leather wallet, subway token, battery, popper, hose clamp, alligator clip, film cartridge, jack (from game of jacks), pocket screwdriver, hook (scissors), Mary Jane sweets, stock cubes, toy bullets, pocket aspirin box, spools of thread, model paint can*, mousetrap, tiny lightbulb, single-edge razor blades (wrapped and unwrapped), more poppers, Monopoly hotel, Life Saver sweets, bottle screw-cap, Scrabble tile, wafer biscuits. **COUNTER AREA:** Lipstick, button (on lipstick)*, package carrying handle, picture hook, book of matches, dungarees buckle, luggage tags. **Deli case:** hinge, shelled peanuts, garter hook, silver coin*, white electrical wire*, light-switch plate, expandable watchband, fuses, crayons, pastels, pink pencil-tip rubber, pebble, stamp-moistening jar, hook (tongs). **RIGHT-HAND DISPLAY TABLES AND STOVE:** Rubber stamps, aspirins (soap), postage stamp, dollar bill, hand grenade, buckles, felt-tip marker, cinnamon sticks, rubber band, tin-can lid*, binder clip, drawer handle. **FOREGROUND DISPLAYS AND MERCHANDISE:** Chessboards (floor). **Counter and basket on left:** fake fingernails, shoelaces*, starfish. **Vacuum cleaner display:** spiral seashell (vase), egg timer, disposable razor, tube of paint, toenail clipper, bulldog paper-clip. **Food table and sacks:** drill chuck, key, wooden beads (cheeses), champagne cork cage, pistachio nuts, beer-mat, peanuts, brass paper-fastener, clothing label.

PARK AND ZOO

• 174 Look-alikes

BUILDINGS IN BACKGROUND: Mosque: coin-roll wrappers, flower bulb, jingle bell*, carpenter's crayon, onion, striped birthday candle, Hershey's Hug sweet. **Green-domed building:** votive candle, Scrabble tiles, dollar bill. **Skyscraper:** ballpoint pen and holder. **Red-roofed building:** pushpins, inflator needle (for blowing up balls, etc.), pen nibs, Christmas lights, three-year chequebook calendar. **Church:** bullets, jack (from game of jacks), watch strap, wheat cracker. **Remaining buildings:** talcum-powder tin, alphabet blocks, felt-tip marker, dice, green pencil-tip rubber, gum rubbers, Monopoly house, baseball-game ticket, fine-line marker, discount theatre ticket voucher, little cardboard box*. **MIDDLE AREA, LEFT-HAND SIDE:** Broccoli, miniature rolling pin, cigar box, combs, maze puzzle, pastels, pretzels, swizzle-sticks, package-carrying handle, cinnamon stick*. **Lamppost:** acorn cap, marble, lipstick brush, foreign coin. **Stairway and park:** croutons, dominoes, penguin sponge, handbag, chocolate squares, Brussels sprout. **PLAYGROUND: Boat pond and tower:** tortilla chip, Lucite artist's palette, birdseed bell, toilet-roll tube, poppy seeds (gravel). **Drinking fountain:** scallop shell, rhinestone earring, chess bishop, foreign coin*, dog treats. **Sandpit and contents:** tambourine, cork, spool of blue thread, green plastic thimble, nappy pin, animal cracker, starfish, breadcrumbs (sand). **Monkey bars:** Ping-Pong bat, hairbands, wooden matches, hoop earrings. **Base of tree near swings:** draughts pieces*, hairpins*. **Swings:** paintbrush, garter hook, pencils, green birthday candles, paper-clips, acorn, wine cork, pistachio nut, dog biscuits, chess knight, blue book. **Clown slide:** game piece (hat), towelling scrunchie (hat frill), vegetable peeler, magnet, paper clamps, sweet cake decorations, shoehorn, paddle-ball toy. **Fence area:** wooden coat-hangers, hair-grips, black crayons, drill bits, kidney beans. **Lamppost:** Christmas ornament, brass doorknob, champagne cork cage. **Bench and squirrel:** melba toast, wall hooks, pussy-willow catkin, chocolate biscuit (drain cover). **ZOO:** Basket. **Antelope and its house:** red pick-up stick, wallet, popcorn, sweetcorn kernels, spotted spiral seashell, Brazil nuts. **Ostrich and its pen:** fan-shaped brush, rubber bands, clothes-pegs, wooden combs, pale blue egg. **Birdcage and its inhabitants:** miniature paper umbrella, almond in its shell, coffee bean*, burnt paper matches*, hooks (hook-and-eye type)*, pine cone*, salted sunflower seeds*. **Tree:** pineapple top. **Giraffe:** rubber fingertip, alphabetti spaghetti*, more sweetcorn kernels, grain of rice (eyelid), piece of twine, jigsaw puzzle pieces. **Gate:** windscreen wiper, watch strap, black buttons, sewing-machine bobbin, black chess pawns, embroidery scissors, pairs of compasses with pencils, fine-point pens, striped sunflower seed. **IN THE PATHWAY: Gazebo:** badminton shuttlecock, cigarettes. **Tree:** brown leather glove. **Lamppost:** black chess pawn, toy ring in plastic bubble from vending machine, ballpoint pen with cap, doorbell. **Ice-cream man, his cart and customers:** key-chain clasps (his coin holder)*, nail, nappy pins, single-edge razor blades, tapestry sewing needle, tea-light, supermarket bonus stamp, metal thimble, tiny padlock, dried maple-seed case (girl's ponytail). **Bicycle:** eyelash curler, magnifying glass, poppers. **Fountain, plaza and angel:** acorn, screw, dried maple-seed case (angel's sleeve), seashell, fuse, drinking glass, hose nozzle, juicer, crystal ash-tray, pretzels, popcorn, black-eyed peas, pennies, (more poppy seeds).

AMUSEMENT PARK

• 119 Look-alikes

CASTLE: Tiny darts, ice-cream cones (two types), toy trumpet Christmas ornament, brass hose nozzle, spool of red thread, tiny stud earrings, swizzle-stick (flagpole)*, penny, plastic squeeze bottle, white dominoes, honey dipper, plastic nozzle, clothes-pegs, pink pencil-tip rubbers, striped wallet, chess bishop, coin-roll wrapper, party horn, magnet, book, broccoli, pearl earring. **FOUNTAIN:** Baby teething ring*, Christmas lights, paintbrushes, spiral seashell. **RIDES IN BACKGROUND: Ferris wheel:** scissors, binder clips, embroidery hoops, hair perming rods, yellow plastic cocktail forks*, pick-up sticks, pencil-sharpener, garden fork, pocket comb, Afro picks. **Roller coaster:** guitar, toothpicks. **Moon shot:** cake decorator, takeaway coffee-cup lid. **Dragon and its ticket booth:** clamp, pair of compasses, pliers, autumn oak leaves, miniature paper umbrella, tiny buckle. **"Wild West" exhibit:** postage stamps. **Smaller wheel on right:** dartboard, nutcracker, black dominoes*. **RIDES AND ATTRACTIONS IN MIDDLE DISTANCE: Carousel:** bell, toy crown, jam jar, peanuts (horses), bicycle sprocket. **Kiosk:** jingle bell,

red stick for homemade ice lolly. **Ticket booth:** cupcake case, another tiny buckle, rubber band*. **Daffy Discs:** pencils, suction-cup dart, silk daffodils, big red buttons, record, Frisbee*, plastic sword toothpicks. **Balloon seller:** ball-headed straight pins. **Topsy Turvy:** spinning top, tubes of paint, guitar picks, sequins (propellers), hair-grips, gold necklace. **Circular ride behind boy:** tambourine, juicer, keys, retractable tape measure*. **BOY ON RIDE:** Silk autumn maple leaf, twirler's baton, suitcase. **BOOTHS AND STRUCTURES IN FOREGROUND: Game booths:** knitting-needle, cap-gun caps, Chinese finger puzzle, more peanuts (teddy bears), thimble, pearls, chess pawns, tickets, cigarette-lighters, (Note: Guatemalan "worry dolls" are miniatures rather than look-alikes), fish-hooks, crayon. **Candyfloss booth:** yellow pencil-tip rubber, tiny toy rabbit, spotted seashell, tip of crayon, nailbrush, price tag, photographic slide holder, chewing-gum in wrapper*, cotton buds, pink rubber, votive candle. **Children's ball jump:** sink plug, billiard ball, pot holder weaving loom, rolls of streamers, parakeet perch with bells, pearl anklet, jelly beans. **Behind ball jump:** tyre pressure gauges, combs, pretzel sticks, spiral notepad. **"Test Your Strength"**: meat thermometer, playing-cards*, milk bottle lid. **On ground:** leather glove, spices.

HOTEL

• 129 Look-alikes

TOP OF WALL: Spool of thread*, wooden spoons, cardboard matches, accordion peg coat rack, unbleached coffee filters, wine cork, pretzels, yardsticks, folding knives (archway on right). **SHOP WALL ON LEFT:** Five-dollar bill, jigsaw puzzle pieces, doorstop, plastic spiders, cigarillos, brass letter *T*, bubble wrap, small screwdriver, tiny buckle (doorknob plate)* (Note: Tiny bottle is a miniature rather than a look-alike), playing-card, spiral seashell, golf tee. **BACK WALL:** Chocolate bars, crayons. **Marble pillars:** buttons, map sections, rubber bands*, custard creams. **Arch:** fancy hair clip. **Sculpture on wall:** polished pebble, beige chess pawns, spiral biscuits, sweetcorn kernel, night-light fixture, *biscotto* biscuit. **On stairway wall:** feather fishing lure, stone arrowhead, embroidery hoop, artificial leaf, shade pull, pencils. **On upper landing wall:** tea ball, metal book-end, cat litter scoop, squishy fish fishing lure, cup hook, pine cone*. **RESTAURANT:** Lace fan, white nylon gloves, six-pack plastic rings, toy green plastic dinosaurs, crystal doorknob, toilet plunger, small wooden scoop, hairpins, cupcake cases, tiny artificial flowers (lamp-shades)*, brass paper-fasteners (vases)*, acorn (chicken), thimble, nail-brush. **OBJECTS IN FRONT OF BACK WALL:** Razor, crossword puzzle, bullets, gold-toned coins*, meat thermometer, hoop earring, hose nozzle, comb, wheat crackers, rubber stamp, Christmas bauble, chess knight, jumbo pavement chalk, wooden crochet hook, plastic cock-tail forks, shaving brush, ivory-coloured dominoes. **HANGING LAMPS:** Ballpoint pen with top, doorbell, candle, bicycle sprocket, silk flowers. **LOUNGE AREA:** Pennies, pen nib, peat pot, tiny gold safety-pins, penknife, pea pods, ceramic napkin ring, coin purse, hair-grips (on front of chair arms)*, restaurant coffee creamer, salt shaker, shoe-polish tin, lamp socket, orange suede gloves, postage stamps, picture-frame, spool of gold thread, gold-foil-wrapped chocolate coin, bars of soap (two sizes), camouflage cloth, autumn leaves, dried maple-seed cases, doilies, red and natural pistachio nuts, feathers. **RECEPTION AND LIFT AREA:** Silver peppermill, lavender ponytail elastic*, black chess pawn, oven thermometer, old-fashioned key, museum admission tag, marble-based desk pen set, peacock feather*, leather wallet, chopsticks, unopened tube of flypaper, dog chews, toggle buttons, nutmeg grater, plastic protractor, window lock, clear ballpoint pen, table knives, silver crochet hook, wooden switch plate, single-edge razor blades, card of drawing-pins.

NEIGHBOURHOOD

• 98 Look-alikes

PHARMACY BUILDING: Crackers, folding carpenter's ruler, dollar bill, paintbrushes, candle, electrical plug, sunglasses, postage stamp, worry doll, single-edge razor blade*, white button, plastic skull, Smarties*, stick of chewing-gum in wrapper*, toothbrushes, ballpoint pens, dental floss container*, card of drawing-pins. **JUANITA'S BODEGA BUILDING:** Pistachio nuts, dog biscuits (two sizes), wooden matches, hoop earring, corrugated cardboard, thimble, rubber stamp*, yellow stick for homemade ice lolly (lamp), Goldfish crackers, sweetcorn kernels, taco shell, sugar birthday cake letters, birthday candles, corn-on-the-cob holders, tape measure, plastic protractor, pretzel, package carrying handle, pencils, orange button (door-knob), picture hook, nappy pin, bottle of pickled chillies, part of wallet (door)*, miniature watercolour set, wristwatch, seashell. party blow-out toy, yellow button, (another worry doll), Cheerio, red electrical connector, embroidery floss, cranberries, popcorn, clothes-pegs. audio cassette, postage stamp, chewing-gum pieces, number puzzle. **PARK AREA:** Kale, broccoli, package wrapped in grey paper and white string, book, flat-leaf parsley*, pretzel sticks, saltshaker, white chalk, wooden blocks, popcorn, crayons, keyhole pliers, key, ballpoint pen refill, stick of gum in wrapper, cut pencils. **MURAL AND SKYSCRAPER:** Jigsaw puzzle piece, pink glove, skeleton emblem, graph paper. **BAKERY BUILDING:** Kidney beans, melba toasts, tartan shoelace, ruler, cap-gun caps, pair of compasses, red shoelace*, tan chess pawn*, baby-bottle teat, clear plastic change purse, pistachio nuts, penny, bar of soap, birthday candles. **PAVEMENT AREA:** Slices of bread, tortilla chip, baby dummies, bulldog paper-clips*, blue drinking straw, screwdriver, olive with pimento.

SWEET SHOP

• 117 Look-alikes

CEILING AND WALLS: Dollar bills, takeaway coffee-cup lids, baby-bottle teats, shade pull, plastic cocktail forks, playing-cards, cat litter scoops, small old-fashioned key, restaurant order pads, drinking straws, button, sword toothpicks. **BOOTH AREA:** Books, saltshaker (lamp), paintbrushes, lanyard clasps, acorn cap, Afro picks, fig bars, pocket calculator, toenail clipper, supermarket bonus stamp, electronic connectors (vases), cigar holder, bottle cap, fish-hook, number puzzle, travel chessboard. **Jukebox:** toy pilot's wings, plastic protractor, whistle, button*, cold capsules in wrapper, pencils, egg slicer. **Small cabinet:** hair-grip, birthday candles, tiny light bulbs, matchboxes, sweetcorn kernels, clothes-pegs, safety-pins, toy car, gum rubbers. **SODA FOUNTAIN, BEHIND THE COUNTER:** Wooden clothes hanger, pennies, old-fashioned key, scallop shell, toy compass, bottle stoppers, penknife, chopsticks, yardstick, chess pawns, package carrying handles, cigarillos, ballpoint pens, compact discs, drop earring, night-light fixture, guitar finger pick, postage stamps, clear pushpins, anchovy tin*, orange crayon, bells, bottle cap, spark plug, thimble, bamboo beads, bingo call number, luggage tag, coin changer, harmonica, fuse, fondue fork (towel rack)*. **COUNTER AREA:** Stock cube, wedding ring, book of matches, overalls buckle, matches, red and yellow crayon tips, pencil-sharpeners, two small padlocks, tiny spiral seashells, birthday-candle holder, blue magnifying glass (pie plate)*, buttons (pie)*, retractable measuring tape, ballpoint pen refills, cocktail forks, another old-fashioned key, unwrapped sticks of chewing-gum, blue knitting-needle, dried apricots, silver dollars, brass hose nozzles, coffee beans (girl's ponytails). **FOREGROUND:** LP record, dominoes, pretzels, pretzel sticks, round crackers, tea-tin lids, baby-bottle teats, garter hook, digital clock, pen nibs, clear plastic purse, leather wallet, tapestry sewing needle, crochet hook, powder puff (left-hand cake), pan of watercolour paint, white poker chip (middle cake plate)*, party streamer roll, six-inch clear plastic ruler.

CIRCUS

• 113 Look-alikes

TENT: Trenchcoat, pair of trousers, large zip (on right), American flag (partly behind band), small plastic bandage, paper doll's outfit, fish-hook with lure, silver evening bag*, pearl sweater clasp. **TENTPOLES, RIGGING, AND LIGHTS: Up high, left to right:** pairs of compasses with pencils, garter hook, TV antenna, red and blue valve handles, arrows, two skirt hangers, covered hook-and-eye, alligator clips*, knitting-needles, hoop earrings*, large hair-grip, safety-pins, lanyard clasp, beaded chain (trapeze artist's ladder), carpenter's clamp, beaded necklace (trapeze artist's rope), domino, door latch hook, drop earring, sewing needle, cheese slicer, yardstick (tent pole, right foreground). **Trapezes:** cord necklace with pendant, hair-grip, glasses strap, cotton bud. **Lower down, left to right:** bulldog paper-clips, key holder, keys, artist's paintbrush, silver pencil-sharpener, bike reflector, pencils, fish hook and lure, chopsticks, gold-edged ribbon (ladder), brass paper-fasteners, corn-on-the-cob holders, M&Ms, tap aerator, vegetable peeler, blue pencil-tip rubbers, snooker-cue chalk, toy googly eyes, aspirins, (another fish-hook and lure), hook (hook-and-eye type), binder clips. **Technician's platform:** pushpins, wristwatch face, blue pet halter, bottle cap, roll of film, paper clamp*, track for model train. **SURROUNDING THE RING:** Striped birthday candles, alphabet stencils, audio-cassette, matchboxes, matches. **Band:** paper-fastener box, eye-shadow applicator, spools of thread. **Entrance-way:** model train boxcar, party blow-out toys, star-shaped candle holder, small yellow candle, peacock feathers, tiny gold safety-pins, dollar bill (rug). **Calliope:** toy flutes, protractor, pen nibs, flagpole finial*, toy bullet, old-fashioned key, yellow paper-clips, sweetcorn kernels, penny, harmonica, binder clip (hitch). **RING AREA AND PERFORMERS: Animal stands:** cat toy, cupcake case, rubber band, hosiery garter, wooden block (far right). **Ring:** tickets, cap-gun caps, straw place mat, patchwork hot pad, champagne cork cages. **Baby carriage:** miniature cheese, hook (hook-and-eye type), green buttons. **Springboard:** artist's sandpaper pad, silver popper. **Floor:** silk scarf, paper bags. **Clown:** tiny spiral seashell, ponytail elastic, tubes of paint. **Trapeze artist:** fake fingernails. **Harlequin girl:** towelling scrunchie, purple silk flower, garlic cloves.

HARBOUR

• 113 Look-alikes

BACKGROUND BUILDINGS: Fancy canister. **Brown building:** whisk broom, clipboard, brown crayons, fondue forks, coin, cigarillos. **In front of brown building:** bricks, jumbo pavement chalk, talcum-powder tin, felt-tip pen cap, wooden comb, chess king, alphabet block. **Dark green building:** cow bell, insulated staples, book. **To right of dark green building:** folding carpenter's ruler, level, blackboard rubber, striped wallet, CD cases, rubber stamp, pocket calculator, fig rolls, egg slicer, address book with pencil, silver thimble, size/price-tag, felt-tip marker, (more alphabet blocks). **WATERFRONT STRUCTURES: Left-hand loading dock:** mailbox (with red flag partly raised), wheat crackers, red zip pull, cup hook, craft knife, finishing nail, drop earring, pair of compasses with pencil, pepper packets, toy giraffe, tiny poppers, cap-gun caps, unwrapped cough-drops, unwrapped sticks of chewing-gum, cutting board with built-in knife, cinnamon sticks. **Grey loading dock:** coin, pencil, wrapped sesame snaps, matchbox, small black button. **Ferry building and dock:** pliers, disposable razors, toy compass, cuff-link, tape measure. **Gas storage tank:** sugar shaker, admission ticket. **Buildings near ocean liner:** pocket aspirin box, toy baby bottle, gum rubber, battery, audio cassette, artist's sandpaper pad (pier), green party rattle, steel hinges. **BRIDGE AND SUPPORTS:** Brown plastic doorstop, nutcrackers, windscreen wipers. **FAR SHORE:** Natural sponges, book of matches, pencil-sharpener, blue birthday candle, dominoes, plastic lizard. **BOATS: Boat docked at left:** canned ham, brass paper-fastener*, sewing-machine bobbin with red thread, wing nut. **Docked cargo ship:** nail clipper, bottle cap, pistachio shells, pair of compasses, crochet hook, spool of white thread, lipstick, old-fashioned towel rack, sewing-machine bobbin (on mast), heel protector*. **Ferry:** nailbrush, scrubbing brush. **Ocean liner:** steam iron, dice, white domino, disposable lighters, key*, white pushpin, upside-down miniature figure. **Ship under bridge:** bottle/can-opener. **Sailboat:** guitar pick, sewing needle*. **Tugboat:** doll's shoe, inflator needle. **Departing ship in foreground:** mandolin, Life Saver sweet, burnt matches, black chess pawn, doorstop, wooden coat-hanger, cigarettes. **WATER:** Blue lace, white lace, cut-off crayons (buoys).

JOAN STEINER

is a graduate of Barnard College in New York City and a self-taught artist. Her unique three-dimensional creations have appeared in *The New York Times*, *Games Magazine*, *Nickelodeon* and *Sesame Street Magazine*. The recipient of numerous art and design awards, including a Society of Illustrators Award and a National Endowment for the Arts fellowship, Joan lives in Claverack, New York.